PORTOBELLO SONNETS

Harry Clifton was born in Dublin in 1952, but has travelled widely in Africa and Asia, as well as more recently in Europe. He won the Patrick Kavanagh award in 1981 and has been the recipient of fellowships in Germany, France, the United States and Australia.

He has published seven collections of poems, including *The Desert Route: Selected Poems 1973-88* and *Night Train through the Brenner*, all from Gallery Press, with *The Desert Route* co-published by Bloodaxe Books in Britain. *On the Spine of Italy*, his prose study of an Abruzzese mountain community, was published by Macmillan in 1999. A collection of his short fiction, *Berkeley's Telephone*, appeared from Lilliput Press in 2000. His previous collection of poems, *Secular Eden: Paris Notebooks 1994-2004*, was published by Wake Forest University Press in 2007 and won the *Irish Times* Poetry Now Award. His latest titles are *The Winter Sleep of Captain Lemass* (2012), shortlisted for the *Irish Times* Poetry Now Award, *The Holding Centre: Selected Poems 1974-2004* (2014), and *Portobello Sonnets* (2017), all published by Bloodaxe Books in Britain and Ireland and by Wake Forest University Press in the USA.

He has taught in Bremen and Bordeaux universities, as well as Trinity College and University College Dublin. He returned to Ireland in 2004. He was Ireland Professor of Poetry in 2010-13.

Harry Clifton

PORTOBELLO SONNETS

BLOODAXE BOOKS

Copyright © Harry Clifton 2017

ISBN: 978 1 78037 347 8

First published 2017 by
Bloodaxe Books Ltd,
Eastburn,
South Park,
Hexham,
Northumberland NE46 1BS,
and by Wake Forest University Press in the USA.

www.bloodaxebooks.com
For further information about Bloodaxe titles
please visit our website or write to
the above address for a catalogue.

Supported using public funding by
ARTS COUNCIL
ENGLAND

Cover design: Neil Astley & Pamela Robertson-Pearce.

Printed in Great Britain by Bell & Bain Limited, Glasgow, Scotland, on
acid-free paper sourced from mills with FSC chain of custody certification.

PORTOBELLO SONNETS

Portobello (Irish *Cuan Aoibhinn*, meaning 'beautiful harbour'): A Dublin area stretching west from Richmond Street as far as Clanbrassil Street, bordered on the north by South Circular Road, on the south by the Grand Canal. Victorian redbricked houses for the middle classes on the larger streets, and terraced housing by the canal for the working classes. Towards the end of the 19th century, an influx of Jews, refugees from East European pogroms, gave the name 'Little Jerusalem' to the area.

PORTOBELLO SONNETS

In the third age, we are content to be ourselves,
however small.

PATRICK KAVANAGH

1

Dublin under sea-fog, dreeping weather —
Salt air blown inland... The cab turns west
At Brady's pharmacy, into the nightlit drizzle
Of Harrington Street. And now for the acid test —
Alive to the danger, in this monkey-puzzle
Of ancestry, this maze of one-way streets,
Are you not scared, young man, of your Daddy's ghost
And his before him, waiting here to greet you,
Latest of blow-ins, ready to try again?
Is this where you get off, where the heart still melts
For the millionth time, old snow becoming rain
Off the Irish Sea — a flat in the Jewish quarter?
Immerse yourself, disturb the human silt,
An anchor feeling for bottom, in home waters.

2

Look me up, with the blind, the lame and the halt
At Leonard's Corner. Any day of the week
You may see me there, malingering without guilt
At the heart of things, on a coffee break,
Nothing more in mind than how not to die
At the terrible intersections, changing lights –
Old woman, help me across! Blind man, light my way! –
Beyond the window, through the needle's eye
To the only freedom middle age permits:
To taste strange apples, browse
In the junkshop of religion, and buy stained glass
By the fragment, where the vision splits –
Jerusalem / Babylon – down Clanbrassil Street,
From Laura Jane to Bismillah Rice and Meat.

3

Overnight snow in the east. Already a thaw
By morning, and the blown grey smoke
Of dissipating cloud-cover, natural law
Unveiling itself, made infinite by the shriek
Of a seagull, a few rooftops, the steeples
Of two churches. Slowly the sun
Irradiates, warms. But where are all the people?
Why has the city shrunk to a point? I run
To overtake the moment, without ever moving
From the window-seat, or breaking out
In any kind of sweat, lest the will take over.
Listen, sit, be grateful for a day
When nothing happens. Time, pure light
And silence, the world looking the other way.

4

Tell me, does anyone ever get blind drunk
Around here, and spew their guts out
Somewhere along Victoria, Stamer Streets
At three in the morning? Is there a brink?
An abyss? Joe Edelstein, crossed in love,
You who smashed the glass on a fire alarm
For a night in prison years ago, what do you think?
Is there a special hour for crossing over?
Is there a special cell where the soul keeps warm?
Tonight on Lennox Street, the shadows flit
From nothing to nothing. Strange, the faceless pools
Dissolve and gather, not looked into
Except by the sick at heart – the renegade souls,
Internal exiles, tapping at frightened windows.

5

How to survive the dangerous Dublin stretch,
To sing, as Beckett says, in the last ditch
That calls itself Ireland? Think, for instance, of Krapp
Outside his mother's window, on the canal,
Watching the blinds come down. That hospital,
Does it still exist? That safe maternal lap,
Was it ever there to begin with? Second self,
To get through all of *that*, let's strip the shelves
Of alcohol, and drink the Lower Deck dry,
Anaesthetise ourselves, in the jaundiced eye
Of regulars, as the plank floor
Tilts against us, and their terrible laughter
Rings in our ears, and we make it through the door
To the clarity and peace of the morning after.

6

The envelope, bright yellow or bright blue,
With anything positive – that's the one I want
Slipped under my door. Electrifying news
Out of nowhere! The earthly honour, the grant
From the powers-that-be, the trickle-down
From infinity, that pumps like a blood transfusion
Through the psyche. Whites and browns,
The dry rejection note, the kind but useless
Invitations, by the day, to be a face in the crowd
At someone else's triumph – bin, don't shelve!
Eleven already, nothing coming through –
No energy, no food for the higher self.
Outside, the deep illusory blue,
The sun that was never yellow, the actual cloud.

7 (Death of an Editor)

There was that green letterbox, and those particular trees
On Harrington Street. I would stop
Whole minutes at a time, before letting it drop,
My envelope, to a world behind the mirror, where no one replies...

That was our contact point. The soul and its farther shore.
I imagined you out there, sifting good and bad,
Your huge indifferent slush-pile, like a god
Moving mountains, though unfortunately, not as immortal.

Thank you from the human world, of 'almost but not quite...'
For the years of intensified waiting,
The depths of disillusionment, and the incidental joys

Of that Synge Street corner, where I sound your Last Post
On a silent trumpet, among children's cries,
New life, new continuities, now, at the end of our tryst.

8

The man in here, demanding time and silence,
Is your husband, my dear, the ne'er-do-well
In the sunlit forenoon, with his coffee and black bile –
The private, the obsessional.... From his cell
He hears you deal with the world, on the telephone,
Moving about, one-handed, while you cook
With the other, and toe a rag on the kitchen tiles.
You would think, wouldn't you, there are enough books
End to end, to block the passage of light
Forever, into the darkened mind
Of one such as he, unable even to write,
Who 'listens inwardly', ever alert to the smell
Of mushrooms, bacon – *don't throw out that rind!*
Is he the chooser? The chosen? Who can tell...

9

When you emerge from the other end of books,
The man on the street will still be there
With his large unanswered question, shattered look
From too much living.... Take the air
From whatever it is you do to make the time
Run backward, against schedules, against night
Without end, when nothing will have a name
And no one will read or write.
He will catch the bus for Limekiln Avenue
With a million others, a face in the rain
From a passing window, off a diminishing queue.
Do they read out there, in the land of Terminus,
Or wipe their feet, struck dumb at the threshold of pain,
And cross forever, dead to all discussion?

10

They frighten me slightly, those nice boys and girls
Who never put a foot wrong, whom Plato himself
Would have left to write their poems, in his ideal world
With the demons gone. I take them off the shelf
In wonderment – technical brilliance, youth, *élan*,
The sons and daughters, everywhere applause
For their liberal struggle, against known odds,
Their victory. I shut them again and pause.
Outside is loneliness, death, the night of the gods
Who never came back in time, to make the difference
That saves or destroys, but always authenticates
The acolytes. We are doomed, my dear,
And no one to speak up, in our defence.
Turn out the light, take off your clothes, come here....

11

Who was it said we're born in the second act?
Well, this is still the first one. Captain Boyle,
His wife between the sheets, and the odds stacked
Against him, calls the bluff of one and all.
Cigars, champagne, a three-piece suite
On hire purchase. Not to see, that's strength –
To keep the terrible world at arms length
For half a lifetime… Rioters in off the street,
West Dublin voices, all-too-real,
Departing from the script, through the double-glaze
Breaking and entering *Crash!* – the shabby genteel,
Our alter egos, living as we do
In stewardship, my love, of unreal space
That was never ours, in terror of Act Two.

12 *(To the singer Freddie White)*

You went away and sang to the Boston Irish,
Now you're back. 'Like playing at a riot...'
Maybe, but not here, among the old crowd
At Whelan's, on a typical Tuesday night,
With a set-list from the eighties, rain outside,
And favourites being called for. Who survives?
Friends out of rehab – Duhan, Hiatt.
Second marriages – Newman, Earle. Who died?
Frank Zappa, prostate cancer. Waller, Kern,
So long ago their legacy arrives
Like light from outer space. The universe too
Has its supporting acts, in this case you
On the human stage. Admissions, no returns.

13

Linoleum, yellow light – the Noodle House
On Wexford Street. A woman, arm in sling,
In conversation with her latest squeeze
On leave from the cause… Invisible, all-seeing,
If the gods had any use for me
But jealousy, I would die to tell her story.
For I know that girl. Her beauty, her ideals
Born after me, and doomed to die before me.
Years will pass. It will grow unreal,
The room they share above a wholesale butcher,
Marx, Red Shelley and the people's future
Dreamed, unrealised…. I see it all –
Linoleum, yellow light, the sex-appeal
Of a broken arm, the politics of a fall.

14

Rogue narcissus, how did you get in there
Among the daffodils, exfoliating
Whitely on your own, where sill and chinaware,
Islands of six-pronged yellow, soundless, weightless,
Give themselves so blindly to the light?
In a world of objects, does the second self
Stop once too often, take from a shelf
A favourite book, stay mesmerised by the shape and quiet
Of the room it glides through, palpable time
Personified, unstoppering whole jars
Of mindblowing essence, starting its own church –
*O multiple fragrance, egotistical sublime
Intensified! O narcissistic flower!* –
One afternoon, in the headlong riot of March….

15

Clouds, too, are incoming information.
Here I am, interrogating silence
As the saying goes, the soul on trial
In the ever-changing light of contemplation.
Glad enough that someone, through the wall,
Is doing the opposite. Skyping, taking calls
And digiting at intervals between,
Unreal friends, on her little silver screen.
The clouds are moving slowly. Green things grow
On both sides of the wall. Am I criminal,
Indifferent, waiting for the other shoe
To fall, as she quietens, finally,
And the sky clears, and the human animal
Caged in both of us relaxes, yawns, feels free?

16

What feeds the secret sources? What
Do the secret sources feed? Are there geese
Like myself, among so many swans
They seem like blow-ins, their trajectories
Broken arcs, their life among the stay-at-homes
Invisible? Have they blown off-course
To winter here? Sit tight, make little poems,
And stroll the grey canal of an afternoon
From Harold's Cross to the opening Red Sea doors
Of Portobello lock, the strait way through
To the Promised Land. There are secret sources,
Pure upwellings. Here though, nothing flows,
Least of all water. Peace, the old repose
Of waiting, the daily door that cannot be forced.

17

Is there a lockkeeper here, who understands
Slow time, changed levels, endlessly being raised
Beyond ourselves? If so, let him show his face
By nightfall – he who broke with wife
And children, took to the waterborne life
And brought us all by leverage through the years
Spent waiting, alien cities, ages
Of horse and diesel, to this desolate landing-stage....
How far inland does it run, the casual writ
He grants himself? On the towpath, women appear
As the lamps come on. A filling station glows
Like civilisation. And the darkness falls
Without intercession – the telephone calls,
The voices, prayers unanswered. No one shows.

18

These are the days that March has lent to April
Under a hard blue dusk of half-lit streets,
A winter retrospective. Give them back
Transfigured, in their winding-sheet
Of white frost, under a brilliant zodiac –
Betelgeuse, Bear and Plough – that lights you home
Past redbrick terraces, the sleepless bric-à-brac
Of children's toys, in see-through living-rooms.
Tomorrow, they will inherit the earth
You and your shadow leave them – reversible days,
The past alive in the present, frostbitten blaze
Of cherry and magnolia, pure self-worth
Dreaming itself all night, at first light coming true
Along Victoria Street, and Bloomfield Avenue.

19

Crunch of a car, in the gravelled yard below,
A rattle of baby carriages. Look out
At the generation forming, the snipped cord,
Ireland drifting away, into a long ago
Policed by myth and terror. New century, new dawn –
And the late-arisen, through the playschool door
Manoeuvring their children. First-time fathers,
Grey already. Women, neither rich nor poor,
Black, yellow and white, still bleary-eyed
From the centuries... This is something else –
Emancipated forenoon, the adulthood
Of the species, pouring its own elevenses,
Breaking bread, in the secular heaven
Of the drop-in centre, the church absolved of hells.

20

Not for us high priesthood, Dan and I –
A deaconate, maybe. Poems, minor orders
In the broad church of creation. Every day
On Camden Street, between murder
And resurrection, naked among wolves,
He walks his greyhound. Floodlit Harold's Cross
His holy ground. And mine the local bars.
Invisible, the surplice of our selves
We wear in secret. Wordlessly we pass
Into each other's lives, Dan Sweetman and I,
On Camden Street. The calendar of saints
Includes us too, without the saintliness.
Should we say hello? We would sooner die,
Bound, as we are, by temporal constraints.

21

With Jeremiah's lamentations sung
For the fall of Jerusalem – theorb, viol, choir –
The shrouds put on and off, the Christ-child hung
And the resurrection over for another year,
The *tenebrae* move in, the shadowy toilers
In the vineyards of the Lord. Johannes Mabickwa,
Patience Sulamati, Nicholas Simbe,
Good west Dublin names, to trim the wick
On a votive lamp, restore the sacred oils
To the Pro-Cathedral. Coinbox, sweepings, palms –
Eternally, it is Sunday afternoon
In Nineteen Fifty. Oliver Mary Taaffe,
With a voice that echoes like the crack of doom,
Inducts three Chinese altarboys, who try not to laugh.

22

The Pope and Rainier dead, Saul Bellow dead –
Vast crowds and silent homage. Closer to home
Pat Pomphrett, halfway along South Circular Road,
Who can barely remember his own name
Or wake in the morning, has me in his sights.
Lords spiritual, lords temporal, men of art
Protect me now, when the verbal shakedown starts.
A grey old day, as ever in these parts –
Church holidays, lost weekends, a void
You could almost touch... Chicago, Monaco, Rome –
The love that moves the sun and the other stars
Has bottled out around here, and the soul-destroyed
Are too far gone to notice. Here he comes,
Lurching towards me, weaving between the cars.

23

Dim snugs, in coloured little towns
Of southwest Ireland... The fleet comes in
Each evening, and the auctioneers stroll down
To price the catch. No losers here, no winners –
Everyone just exists, in a blaze of harbour light,
A state of redemption. It all gets sold,
The ledgers close, and the oceanic night
Takes over. Everyone has drunk their yellow gold
And staggered home. And the whole place sleeps
In the lee of everything. Deep, deep Ireland,
Deep, deep peace... I am there
In spirit, as the small hours creep
On Bloomfield Avenue, saying it like a prayer
With the lost at sea, who never sleep.

24

People I meet, on the blind wheel of fortune,
Ask me in passing, as they go up,
I down, the sliding scale of importance
Known as Dublin, 'How far now to the top?
If I make it through to the heavenly firmament
How will my head survive?' And then they're gone
(They were only acquaintances anyway…) Time I went
Myself, to the honky-tonk zones
Approximate to my station… Africans, Asians –
Bodies for sale, the shirts off the backs
Of wild-card holders. Weird conflations
Of humanity, left high and dry on the shelf,
Unsold, unwanted, brilliant as the Greeks
At deciphering fate, as powerless as myself.

25

I have it in mind, North African gentlemen,
To write you into our own reality
Such as it is. Would you sit there for me
In the window, Al Houari Boumédiène,

Mohammed Mebtouche, Afshan Jilani,
Eyes averted, women kept unseen,
Unsaleables on shelfspace, nothing unclean
In an empty freezer? The colour of money

Means nothing to you, I know, or the death of God.
Time is your real currency, gentlemen,
Who fly your kites behind glass, and trap the sun

In a yellow frontage. Put aside religion,
Rites of slaughter. By your slightest nod
Acknowledge me, eating here in the Camden Kitchen.

26

Sitting still, or hurtling through the noosphere –
What's the difference? Fellow passengers,
Your feet stink, and your meatloaves, cans of beer
Are giving me grief, as we download messages
In the twilit chat-room. Still, you are of this earth,
And the great age of simultaneity
Washing ambient music, virtual space
About your eyes and ears, has yet to claim you.
Eat on. Be grateful your place of birth
Is still your prison. Africans, Poles, Malays,
That's Camden Street outside there, in the rain –
Not a pretty sight. Depressive greys,
Unbeautiful lives. But if, as De Chardin says,
We leave tomorrow, would you not choose to remain?

27

Weeping, I feel better. Then death comes,
Solving everything. With the anger gone
I sit in the afterlife, over coffee and buns,
Seeing into Camden Street, where an old flame
Out of China – we are all in China now –
Sashays past, in denim and high boots.
Eva who once was Haeng, who changed her name
And transmigrated west
Through the soul-realm, slowly unbinding her feet...
She does not see me. I do not exist.
Besides, we each have paddy fields to plough.
I understand, I forgive. I offer it up
In lieu of earthly payment, to the angel
Who waits tables, the bottomless coffee cup.

28

'I saw an extraordinary thing, the other day.
A girl from Lithuania, staring across
The canal, at a huge mess
Of sticks and bulrushes, caked mud and clay,
Where two swans nested...' Watcher, cob and pen,
Today they are at it again
As I pass with the traffic, in brilliant Spring weather
On Grand Parade – half-hypnotised, each by the other.
All that remains for us is to wheel our bed
Into the street, make love and incubate poems
Right there in public, as the lily pads
Bloom on the surface, the tramlines *ping!*
And Lithuania, of the shattered homes
And cast-out women, takes us under her wing.

29 *(For Marina, who cut my hair)*

Belonging as she did, to the era after the book
And I to the era which, without the book,
Would be unliveable, what we had in common,
This gorgeous blonde-haired woman

From Lithuania and I, was the mirror between us,
Where the left hand and the right
Were privy to each other, but only in God's sight,
And our respective demeanours

Gave away nothing, all those years
Of high communion, silence, fallen hair….
They say she is in India now, or Mexico somewhere

Seeking God. At the hour of her setting-forth
Where was I? Breath on the mirror
Clouds her face. A spirit has strayed from the earth.

30

Ask yourself, as you struggle with your pen
And the light of reason, from over the road
In Bloomfield Motors, streams right into your head –
Have you ever seen a happier bunch of men?
Their music is garage, their blue-lit jokes
Hydraulic, as they tinker with undersides,
Body parts, and the blackened, burnt-out wrecks
Of overnight derangements, underworld rides.
Tonight, the men of bronze go on past twelve
For sheer enjoyment – crankshafts, piston rings,
The fantail of sparks, the water blaster
Sluicing the hide of Plato's social beast
At its most metallic – happier in themselves
Than poet-daemons, rich philosopher-kings.

31 *(The Night Bakery)*

None of them are angels, all wear white,
Their light ablaze on Lennox Street, at the hour
Of breadmaking.... Where does the time go,
Anyone might ask himself, standing here
As I do, between night and morning, heaven and hell,
Breathing it in, the yeasty smell
Of everydayness, freshness for the soul
That only asks of the earth a place to dwell
In weightless ecstasy?
              Batches cool
On the aluminium trays. No price as yet
On anything. Flies are dying, in a blue incandescence.
Somebody steps out for a cigarette.
I watch it being stirred, the mixing bowl
Of spirit and essence....

32

High up here, in the northern latitudes,
First and last light come together
Of a summer night, where a few souls gather
On a cold platform – Harcourt Street
At the witching hour. They are holding the tram
As usual for Grandad, running late
From his job in the Tech, and Daddy with his plans
From the Corporation. Have you found your feet
In the real world, they just have time to ask me
Before the doors close, automatically
And forever.... Desolation and gratitude –
How can I tell them my place is here
Between night and morning, where the human lovers
Kiss goodbye, at the hour of crossing over?

33

Water is there to be looked at, not looked into –
Stay on the surface, where the dragonflies mate,
The girls return your glance, and the weather is great,
And no one gazes through a shattered window
Into the depths. Let the black shapes cruise
Down there, on a backdrop of old news
And drowned ephemera. You can go too deep
And never come back from the realm of archetype.
Once you were like that little boy, with his tin
Of crawling maggots, and his fishing-rod.
Then you committed sacrilege. You looked in,
And saw yourself looming, like the face of God,
Ravaged, hollowed-out, on an infinite sky....
Swim back up to the surface. Live and die.

34

Today I have been a good boy. No harm done
To man or beast. No terrible emanations –
Evil or power. Just sitting in the sun
By the Grand Canal, as relaxation, patience
Without end, for the probably unattainable,
Take over. Nor have I travelled far from home
As once I did, to the lands of sex and pain
Where the muses dwell. Perhaps if I changed my name,
Began again in childhood, the powers-that-be
Would pity me for a schoolboy and a truant,
Leery of institutions, kicking stones
On the towpath, one of those natural loners –
Look at him now, impoverished and free –
Who takes a while to know what he really wants.

35

Even Christ, in his unrecorded years,
Might have lingered here, where Herberton bridge,
Rialto, and the vanished chest infirmary
Kavanagh lay for months in, close to the edge,
Cast their long shadow, from Nineteen Fifty-Five
To this latest of summers, everyone gone
To the wine-dark ocean.... Haunted, the survivor
Walks inland, to pray again at the gates
Of his own deliverance. To come back from the dead,
Just now, is enough. Let anonymity,
Powerlessness, be his lot. The grass that sings
In his ears, the rat hesitating,
Taking him in, a stranger off the sea,
Before they both move on to greater things.

EPILOGUE

William Bates, 1931-2013

About Liam, I know one thing –
He's in tonight, off Richmond Street,
Sipping his infinite pint. A gas-ring
To go home to, body heat,
His own lying-in. A tipstaff
Having the last laugh

On devilling barristers, magistrates
He slaved for… Around here
Of course, he's hated
By the crooked and the straight.
Once, I looked for him
In the pages of Shakespeare,

Found no one. Another time
In the dictionaries –
Not a trace. A man who strayed
From the lore and language of his trade,
Left with only a Christian name.
O Liam, Liam, when you rise

The court is still in session.
There are no goodbyes
For the man in the wrong profession.
I hear you ask 'Is it blowing
Outside?' Old man, forget the assizes –
Where you and I are going

Your walking stick is your staff of duty
And the absolutes, Truth, Beauty,
Goodness, die in the brilliance
Of Richmond Street's crime thriller –
Justice too, your double, rigged
In mace, in periwig.